ANIMALS OF THE WETLANDS

Flamingos

by Karen Latchana Kenney

BELLWETHER MEDIA • MINNEAPOLIS, MN

BLASTOFF! READERS
2

Blastoff! Readers are carefully developed by literacy experts to build reading stamina and move students toward fluency by combining standards-based content with developmentally appropriate text.

Level 1 provides the most support through repetition of high-frequency words, light text, predictable sentence patterns, and strong visual support.

Level 2 offers early readers a bit more challenge through varied sentences, increased text load, and text-supportive special features.

Level 3 advances early-fluent readers toward fluency through increased text load, less reliance on photos, advancing concepts, longer sentences, and more complex special features.

★ **Blastoff! Universe**

Reading Level

Grade **K**

Grades **1–3**

Grade **4**

This edition first published in 2021 by Bellwether Media, Inc.

No part of this publication may be reproduced in whole or in part without written permission of the publisher. For information regarding permission, write to Bellwether Media, Inc., Attention: Permissions Department, 6012 Blue Circle Drive, Minnetonka, MN 55343.

Library of Congress Cataloging-in-Publication Data

Names: Kenney, Karen Latchana, author.
Title: Flamingos / by Karen Latchana Kenney.
Description: Minneapolis, MN : Bellwether Media, Inc., 2021. | Series: Blastoff! readers: Animals of the wetlands | Includes bibliographical references and index. | Audience: Ages 5-8 | Audience: Grades K-1 | Summary: "Relevant images match informative text in this introduction to flamingos. Intended for students in kindergarten through third grade–Provided by publisher"
Identifiers: LCCN 2020033241 (print) | LCCN 2020033242 (ebook) | ISBN 9781644874189 (library binding) | ISBN 9781648340956 (ebook)
Subjects: LCSH: Flamingos–Juvenile literature.
Classification: LCC QL696.C56 K46 2021 (print) | LCC QL696.C56 (ebook) | DDC 598.3/5–dc23
LC record available at https://lccn.loc.gov/2020033241
LC ebook record available at https://lccn.loc.gov/2020033242

Editor: Betsy Rathburn   Designer: Josh Brink

Printed in the United States of America, North Mankato, MN.

Table of Contents

Life in the Wetlands

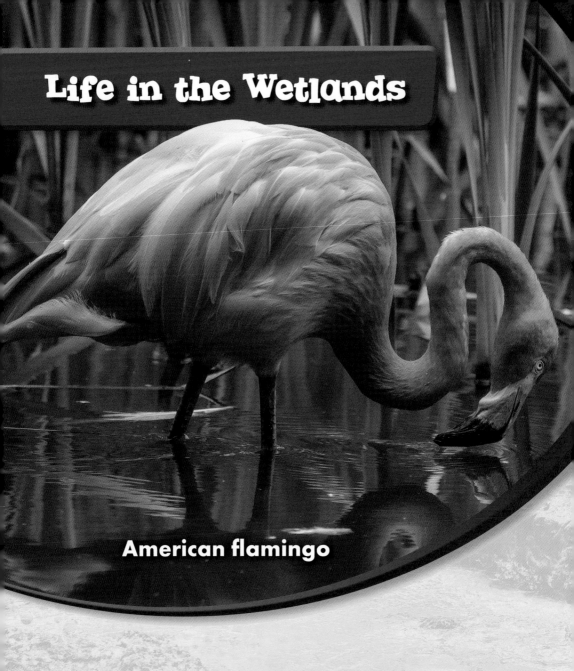

American flamingo

Flamingos are birds known for their pink feathers.

They live in coastal wetlands around the world. They also live in salty lakes in Africa and South America.

American Flamingo Range

N
W ✦ E
S

range = ☐

lesser flamingos

Salty wetlands can be harsh. But flamingos have **adapted** well.

They have **salt glands** on their beaks. These get rid of extra salt!

Flamingos have long, thin legs. They can **wade** through deep water.

Salty water can hurt skin. Thick **scales** protect flamingos' legs.

scales

greater flamingos

Webbed feet help flamingos stay steady in mud.

Their long necks reach far into the water. The birds can get food others cannot!

Special Adaptations

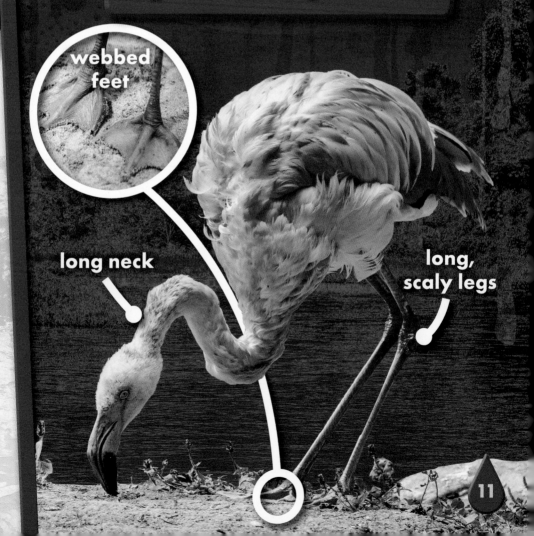

webbed feet

long neck

long, scaly legs

Standing Together

The wetlands are full of **predators**. Flamingos gather in groups for protection.

These huge **flocks** watch and warn each other. Flocks may have thousands of flamingos!

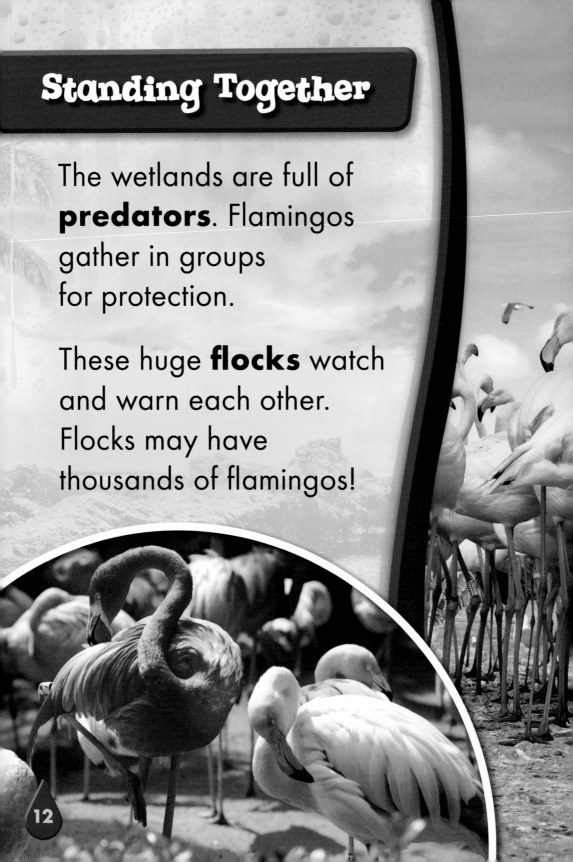

flock

Crowded flocks are loud!
Flamingos must find ways
to **communicate**.

They use **body language** to talk. They **ruffle** their feathers or snap their beaks!

15

Bottom Feeders

The wetlands are full of flamingos' favorite foods. They often eat fish and **crustaceans**.

Flamingos eat a lot of toxic **algae**. This food harms other animals.

American Flamingo Stats

Least Concern	Near Threatened	Vulnerable	Endangered	Critically Endangered	Extinct in the Wild	Extinct

conservation status: least concern

life span: around 40 years

The birds dip their heads
underwater to eat. Their beaks
scoop up muddy water.

Thin plates trap food in their mouths. Mud and water flow out!

Flamingo Diet

brine shrimp

red algae

small fish

Flamingos get their color
from their food. It has a dye
that turns their feathers pink.

These bright birds **thrive** in the wetland **biome**!

Glossary

adapted—changed over a long period of time

algae—plants and plantlike living things; most kinds of algae grow in water.

biome—a large area with certain plants, animals, and weather

body language—a way of communicating using body movements

communicate—to share information and feelings

crustaceans—animals with hard outer skeletons that live in water

flocks—groups of birds that live, travel, or feed together

predators—animals that hunt other animals for food

ruffle—to puff up

salt glands—organs that release salt from the body

scales—small plates of skin that cover and protect an animal's body

thrive—to grow well

wade—to walk through water

webbed—having an area of skin between the fingers or toes

To Learn More

AT THE LIBRARY

Amstutz, Lisa. *Flamingos*. Mankato, Minn.: Amicus, 2021.

Grodzicki, Jenna. *Wild Style: Amazing Animal Adornments*. Minneapolis, Minn.: Millbrook Press, 2020.

Klepeis, Alicia Z. *Flamingos*. Minneapolis, Minn.: Jump!, Inc., 2021.

ON THE WEB

Factsurfer.com gives you a safe, fun way to find more information.

1. Go to www.factsurfer.com.

2. Enter "flamingos" into the search box and click 🔍.

3. Select your book cover to see a list of related content.

Index